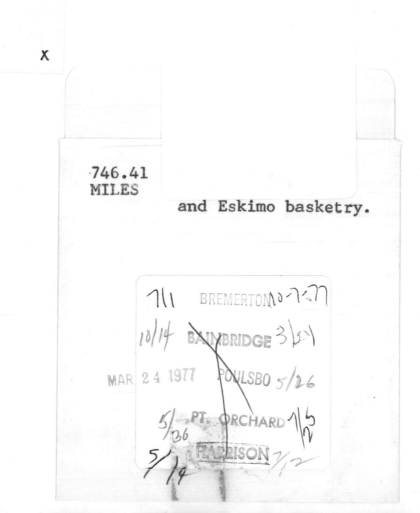

American Indian And Eskimo Basketry

— A KEY TO IDENTIFICATION —

Written and Compiled by
CHARLES MILES and PIERRE BOVIS

BONANZA BOOKS • NEW YORK

ALL THE BASKETS ILLUSTRATED IN THIS BOOK ARE FROM THE AUTHORS' PRIVATE COLLECTIONS, UNLESS OTHERWISE INDICATED.

This book
is dedicated to SYLVIA BOVIS
and JOHN MILES for their help, support
and encouragement

GROUP OF TULARE BASKETS

4

BASKETRY AREAS

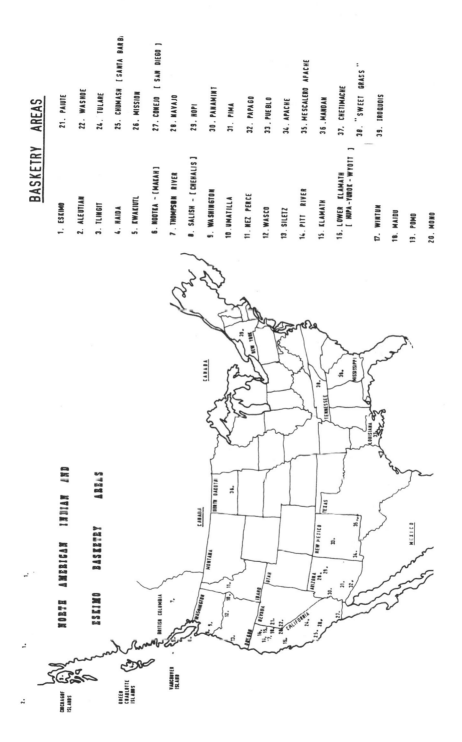

1. ESKIMO
2. ALEUTIAN
3. TLINGIT
4. HAIDA
5. KWAKIUTL
6. NOOTKA - [MAKAH]
7. THOMPSON RIVER
8. SALISH - [CHEHALIS]
9. WASHINGTON
10. UMATILLA
11. NEZ PERCE
12. WASCO
13. SILETZ
14. PITT RIVER
15. KLAMATH
16. LOWER KLAMATH [HUPA - YUROK - WYOTT]
17. WINTUN
18. MAIDU
19. POMO
20. MONO
21. PAIUTE
22. WASHOE
24. TULARE
25. CHUMASH [SANTA BARB.]
26. MISSION
27. CONEJO [SAN DIEGO]
28. NAVAJO
29. HOPI
30. PANAMINT
31. PIMA
32. PAPAGO
33. PUEBLO
34. APACHE
35. MESCALERO APACHE
36. MANDAN
37. CHETIMACHE
38. " SWEET GRASS "
39. IROQUOIS

NORTH AMERICAN INDIAN AND
ESKIMO BASKETRY AREAS

5

CONTENTS

INTRODUCTION

This book has been compiled for those interested in the study and preservation of our American Indian basketry.

As all lovers of this highly skilled art know, the amount of knowledge to be gleaned about it knows no bounderies and one continues with each passing day to discover some new vital scrap of information to help in one's study.

Basketry entered most intimately into the lives of most American Indian tribes and was an essential craft, made use of in clothing (e.g. woven sandals, woven hats); in cooking, storage of grain and water; in carrying both babies in cradles and large burdens of corn, berries, wood, etc.; in their religious ceremonies as gifts and, in the case of death, often exceptionally fine baskets were made for funeral pyres.

We are bringing to you a selection of many kinds of baskets and basketry items from various tribes with clues to their identification.

We do not claim to have accumulated an encyclopedia of information, but feel we have filled a need of the interested student and collector, touching upon most of the major types of basketry.

INDIAN AND ESKIMO BASKETRY

Intended to be a condensed guide to the nature and identity of the basketry artifacts produced by the aboriginal American, the ensuing information will have to omit all but essentials. The reader will then understand that for more than basic facts he can explore elsewhere in more expanded and specialized literature, of which there is plenty, and study collections both in private hands and museums.

Although baskets are the most familiar of basketry products made by the Indians, they are far from being the only basketry items used and other forms of woven objects will be illustrated in this book.

Basketry is a kind of weaving, its simplest form being to put together strands and sticks in such a way as to produce a desired object. In a way, birds' nests are basketry.

The simplest methods used by human beings are plaiting and wicker work, which, incidentally, are used for cloth, only with different, generally limp, materials.

PLAITING is weaving ribbons or strands in and out across other ribbons or threads identical with them or nearly so. In its simplest form it creates a checkered appearance.

WICKER WORK uses a basic "frame", best known as vertical elements which are definitely stiffer than those woven in and out across them; the "frame" being called the "warp" and the more elastic elements, the "woof" or "weft".

TWINED basketry goes a step further and besides the simple in and out weaving, the weft twists or takes a turn around the warp.

As may be supposed, wicker work is considerably stiffer than twined or plaited work as a rule. In fact, it was used in native times for hut, fence and fish weir construction and in modern times is a favorite method for constructing hampers and wastebaskets.

When plaited ribbons are thin strips of wood, they too produce a rather stiff basket, a modern example being some clothes baskets.

These are the three elementary forms of woven basketry, but among the Indians and Eskimos a fourth form was used, which is usually called "COILED", but is sometimes called "SEWN". What corresponds to a warp is a continuous coil of one or more strands of comparatively stiff material, which is fastened into a desired shape with limp strands called "threads" that go round and round two or more thicknesses of coils to hold them tightly in place. As can be understood, it commonly required an awl or needle, hence the word "sewn".

Anyone learning the nature of Indian and Eskimo basketry can tell at a glance which of these four ways was used, though there were many variations within their execution.

The importance of such skill will become apparent as the characteristic appearance of individual tribal or group work is found to vary in their use from area to area in the original America. It is often the first factor in deducing origin. Only one family or tribe produced all four kinds: the Pomo Indians of central western California.

This was appropriate because the area in which basketry was of great importance was roughly from the southern Eskimo country of Alaska in a sweep west of the Rockies around through the Southwest to peter out in the Eastern woodland to a simple minor craft or art, although imprints and charcoal remains indicate it was in pre-Columbian times more important in the Woodlands than it had become at the time of the Discovery.

Besides the method or methods used in a given area of origin, of almost equal and often first importance is the way of decoration. The first Americans, unlike their conquerors, enjoyed art in everything, and regarded everyone as an artist. Basketry was habitually ornamented, all the way from use of the external patterns created by the weaving or coiling, to superimposing a purely ornamental element, such as a nipped-in colored ribbon (imbrication) or strands (false embroidery), feathers, and occasionally beadwork and painting. Using different colored elements was an obvious, hence much used, way to create a pattern or design, and the character of such designs is a third rather easy way to narrow down the origin of a given piece of basketry.

Materials used, is a fourth indicator, but rather difficult in most cases for beginners to recognize — about the easiest being the brown ribbons of cedar bark used in the Pacific Northwest and the ribbons of cane or split wood used in the Eastern Woodlands.

A fifth way to "spot" origin, but requiring some familiarity, can be the nature and form of the artifact. Large conical baskets capable of carrying a considerable load of grain, vegetables or billets of wood, for example, say, "California" and delicate clothlike basketry made of grass is probably Aleutian.

The reader should at this point, and with the aid of illustrative photographs, be able to identify much basketry with a little practice providing he can refer to some identifying characteristics in the following greatly condensed summary of the major distinctive basketry areas. For convenience, we will begin where the material to make basketry dwindles out into the snow and ice of the Polar Eskimo country, and proceed south and east to the Eastern Woodland. (The Plains Indians replaced basketry with leather to a large extent, and the North Woods tribes, with leather and bark).

ESKIMO

Those furthest north produced a somewhat clumsy coiled basketry, surely identified if it has ivory ornaments attached. But in the more forested area, notably along the Kuskokwim River, lots of twined basketry was produced, including socks and mittens to use inside leather counterparts.

ALEUTIAN

Although severely limited by the rather barren nature of their isles, the Aleuts wove some of the finest of all basketry with grass, notably bags and wallets that could be termed "cloth made with grass". A notable ornamentation was with colored yarns and threads originally obtained from the Russians.

TLINGIT

This basketry is quite thin and finely woven, but of inner bark and material more substantial than grass. So-called from the most conspicuous tribe making it, but created by all tribes in the northern part of the area known as the Northwest Coast. It is basically brown, ornamented with brightly colored elements in a technique called "false embroidery" to an extent that makes it one of the most colorful forms of native American basketry. The design or pattern is commonly in ribbons or bands around a cylindrical basket. Once in a while painting is used.

NOOTKA

Also familiar as "Makah", a vigorous Nootka tribe on the coast of Washington (State). This has two forms. The twined basketry is characteristically in diagonal "twists" and has its start at the bottom in checker-plaited weaving. Pictorial designs are common. The plaited form uses rather soft ribbons of bark, frequently in different shades to produce designs, notably to make mats and bags.

SALISH

Also "Thompson River" for British Columbia and "Klikitat" for Washington (State). This is coiled, often so rigid as to sound like wood if struck. Its distinctive surface feature is ornamentation with nipped-in ribbons in natural or dyed colors called "imbrication", a device that quickly identifies the origin.

WASHINGTON

Also called "Salish". This mixes in coiled, but involves local experimentation with twining, a "trademark" being a band of little birds or animals just under the rim.

NEZ PERCE

Notably flat bags with painted or embroidered designs of Plains Indian character. They are called "corn shuck" bags. In this area and on the upper Columbia, women wove and wore a fez-shaped hat.

WASCO

A small tribe in eastern Oregon produced cylindrical bags called "sally bags" with pictorial groups similar to those in the Columbia River pictographs; almost unique in nature.

SILETZ

The only basketry familiarly known as peculiar to Oregon. Its "trademark" is a double handle on baskets.

HUPA

Or "Yurok" or "Wyott", a style used all along the lower Klamath River and in adjacent country. The basketry is best known for small geometrically decorated, bowl-shaped hats or caps and in similarly ornamented cooking and mush bowls; colors — browns, blacks and almost white. Here a peculiar slipper-shaped cradle is a distinctive artifact, the baby being seated on the toe which was filled with moss for reasons known to all mothers and startled fathers.

PITT RIVER

So called because two tribes on that river were its chief exponents. The twined weaving has sharply contrasting black and white geometrical patterns which identify it instantly. An artifact is a conical carrying basket.

KLAMATH

Not to be confused with the Lower Klamath River; the name of a tribe that created a great deal of basketry but, while skilfully made, of a utilitarian nature. Caps had the design showing inside. A gambling tray was the most distinctive artifact.

POMO

The All-Americans of basket makers, tops in skill and outstanding in ornamentation, facile in all weaves and coiling and producers of the spectacular "feather baskets" often completely covered with feathers. To "cover" Pomo basketry is impossible in small space. The Pomos used both coiling and twining well, with a mastery that was equally adept in making baskets the size of a pinhead up to big storage and burden baskets. The women frequently made baskets just for the joy of it, to be gifts or "stunts". The tribe also had its own version of a sit-down baby carrier.

PAIUTE

A general term for tribes in central Nevada.

MAIDU

Similar to Pomo in coiling, hence not easily identified. Also similar to Washoe basketry.

WASHOE

A fine coiled basketry produced in eastern Nevada. A peculiar element in black or red resembling a flame, is a "trademark". A trader once successfully publicized his chief artist so that collectors still seek "Dat So La Lee baskets".

"TULARE"

There was in fact no "Tulare" tribe, but the baskets acquired the general name of "Tulare" because they were made mainly by the Yaudanchi who lived in the upper region of the Tule River, the Koyete, who lived in the middle region and the Wowol who lived in the lower region. These tribes were part of the Yokuts nation which inhabited the San Joaquin Valley.

They produced mostly coiled basketry of a light tawny color base and reddish and/or black decorative designs, usually in stripes. Some common patterns used are called, rattlesnake, ant, and quail designs. A distinctive decoration is a circlet

16

of figures holding hands, popularly identifying a "friendship basket". A basketry jar with a pronounced "shoulder" is a distinctive artifact.

MISSION

So-called because made by tribes in the areas of the old California missions. Similar to "Tulare" but using the design of an interlaced star pattern and some pictorial ornamentation.

PIMA

Most easily identified in shallow coiled bowls with a swirl pattern in black, given to alternating thin and thick ribbony lines, plus frequent use of rectangles.

NAVAJO

Chiefly a bowl used in weddings, having a star design through which a "path" is left to the center.

APACHE

Loosely applied to coiled basketry with black or red ornamentation in geometrical patterns, often sprinkled with figures of persons or animals. Notable artifacts are large jars and bowls. The latter often have a star design. There are several Apache tribes, resulting in a wide variety of designs.

PUEBLO

The Pueblo tribes include the Hopi, Zuni and others. Trays are fashioned of wicker-work and with coiling made with noticably "fat" coils. These tribes also made twined water jars covered with hardened pitch to hold water. Similar water jars and canteens were much used by the Apaches, Pimas, and Paiutes, having the advantage over pottery jars of not being breakable.

MESCALERO APACHE

Using flat fat coils like the Pueblo trays, the Mescalero Apaches of the eastern Southwest made designs using a greenish color, not seen in the other Apache work.

17

CHETIMACHE

The Louisiana tribe most noted for plaited work in checker and twilled patterns using different natural colors of cane "ribbons". As already mentioned, such plaiting was a feature of "modern" Woodland Indian basketry.

"SWEET GRASS"

Another predominantly Eastern Woodland "style" made with coils using stems of grass fastened at intervals with thread, the name arising from the scent of the grass. Long pine needles are also similarly used.

The foregoing "guide" is generally basic but may encourage the new student and collector to study museum collections and the various books on basketry.

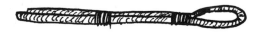

BIBLIOGRAPHY

MASON, Otis Tufton, 1902, *ABORIGINAL AMERICAN BAS-KETRY: STUDIES IN A TEXTILE ART WITHOUT MACHINERY* — Report of the U.S. National Museum.

JAMES, George Wharton, 1902, *INDIAN BASKETRY* A.L. Hettrich and Co., San Francisco, California.

HECKMAN, Albert W., 1919, *INDIAN BASKETRY* — Article from Keramic Studio — a monthly magazine for the potter and decorator

MILES, Charles, 1963, *INDIAN AND ESKIMO ARTIFACTS OF NORTH AMERICA* — Regnery, Chicago

DOUGLAS, H. Frederick, *DENVER ART MUSEUM LEAF-LETS* — Various leaflets

KROEBER & BARRETT, *INDIAN BASKETRY* — University of California, Vol. 2, No. 4

RUSSELL, Frank, 1904-1905, *THE PIMA INDIANS* — Bureau of Ethnology

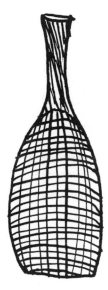

FOUR MAJOR METHODS OF BASKETRY

1. *Plaited;* showing two variations of plaiting and creation of patterns and designs with different shades of (brown) bark and intervals of passing over and under; Nootka, Vancouver Island, Canada.

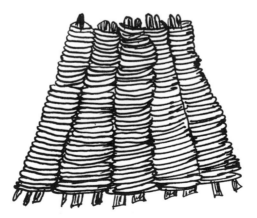

2. *Wickerwork;* radiating rib (warp) work and consequent pattern; also creation of design by colored woof elements; Pueblo, Hopi, Arizona.

23

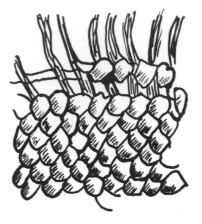

3. *Twined work;* radiation of warp elements seen at bottom, but hidden by the twists of woof in the body; design with black colored woof woven in; woman's hat; northern California.

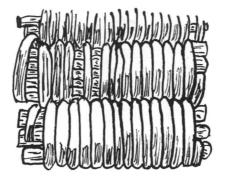

4. *Coiled;* the coiled warp and the stitches around its elements form a continuous spiral; stitches with black strands ("threads") form design; probably Maidu; Sacramento Valley, California.

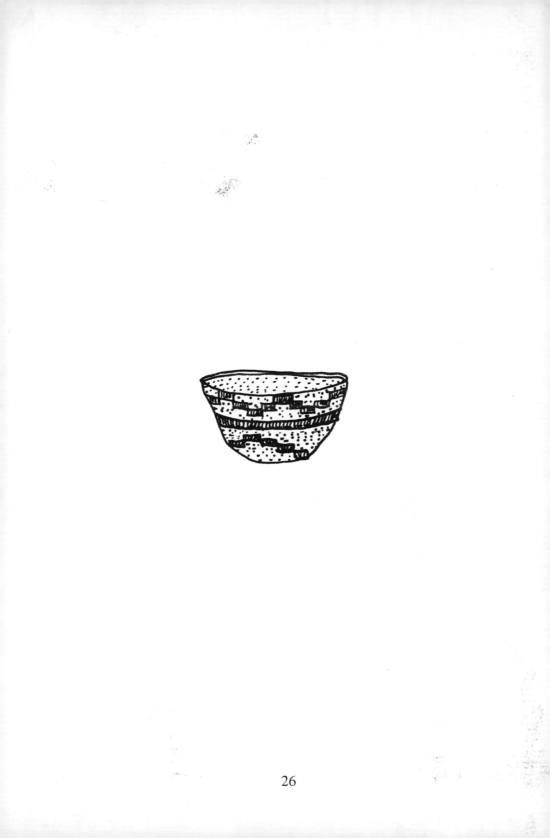

METHODS OF ORNAMENTATION

5. Partially finished twined weave Aleutian wallet, decorated with woven "lace work" and colored silk yarns; Attu Island; dated 1911.

6. "False embroidery"; color elements added, on a Tlingit twined basket; colors usually with native dye but occasionally using analine dyes; Northwest Coast, southern Alaska.

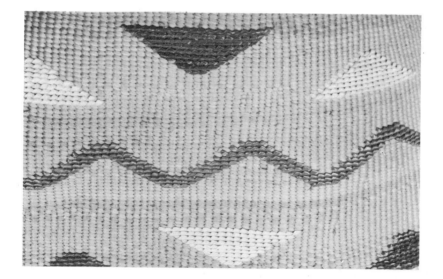

7. Imbrication; bark ribbons of color added and nipped-in on the surface only of a coiled basket; Thompson River, British Columbia.

8. Typical ornamented elements on a Pomo Indian ''gift basket'' (coiled); besides the design made with black on ''straw-colored'' stitching (note regularity), a collar of shell disk beads, danglers of shell and trade beads, and nipped-in feathers (quail top-knots); Russian River and Lake County, California.

31

COMMON UTILITY BASKETS

9. Salish burden basket with widely used openwork. Woven with a stiff vertical warp and double-strand weft twisted at each passage; typical square top, rounded bottom, textile headband attached; northwest Washington.

10. Finely woven, bell-shaped Pomo burden basket in openwork with stiffened round rim; Russian River & Lake County, California.

11. Same kind of Pomo bell-shaped burden basket roughly woven of grape vines; Russian River & Lake County, California.

12. Same type Pomo bell-shaped basket in tight weaving; horizontal weave with vertical ribbing; typical band designs; Russian River & Lake County, California.

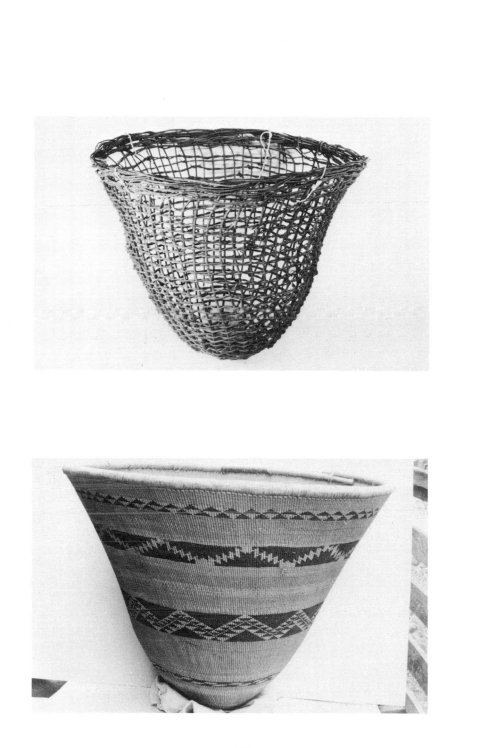

13. Apache burden basket; bottom reinforced with a leather cover and a profuse supply of leather thongs attached; twine weaving; Arizona/New Mexico.

14. Salish coil weave burden basket with cordage for cover fastening; Puget Sound, Washington.

REGIONAL TYPES

15. Open and tight-woven utility baskets of bag type; southern Eskimo.

16. Finely woven, openwork Aleutian utility basket; colored yarn ornaments; Aleutian Islands.

17. Typical cylindrical Tlingit Indian baskets; twined weaving with false embroidery designs; southern Alaska.

18. Typical pictorial Makah basket; black on white background; Nootka style weaving; checker woven base; northwestern Washington.

45

19. Old-style "trinket jar" made by the lower Klamath River tribes; California.

20. Pomo feather and miniature baskets; dime to show scale; Russian River and Lake County, California.

21. Pomo feather and miniature baskets; Russian River and Lake County, California.

22. Pomo feather basket with collar of shell disk beads and quail top-knots; Russian River and Lake County, California.

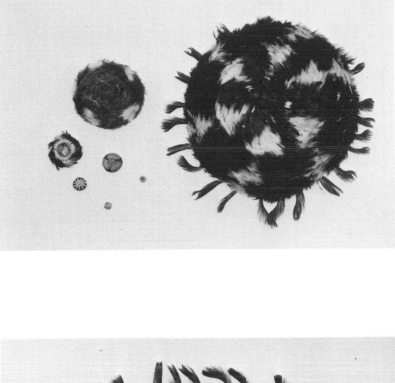

23. Pomo gift basket; ornamental design in coiled work; shell bead collar and bead and shell danglers; Russian River and Lake County, California.

24. Horizontal weave (vertical ribbing) Pomo utility basket; note typical cut-off warp elements on rim; Russian River and Lake County, California.

25. Tulare style jar; rattlesnake banding and "friendship" figures; San Joaquin Valley, California.

26. Chemuevi jar; produced by a small tribe of skilled coil weavers; black designs on white; northern Arizona.

27. Coil weave Hopi plaque portraying a katchina dancer; Arizona.

28. Typical thick coil Hopi tray or plaque with radial design; Arizona.

29. Favorite checker design coiled tray of southwest Indians; Apache; Arizona/New Mexico. (Carol and Doug Allard collection).

30. Plaited weave basket in diagonal technique; this is a Mandan gambling bowl with Plains Indian use of reinforcing wooden ribs at corners; central Plains.

31. Maidu basket; Sacramento Valley, California. (Carol and Doug Allard collection).

32. Apache basket; star design; Arizona/New Mexico. (Carol and Doug Allard collection).

33. Apache basket — bought at San Carlos Apache agency in 1885; Arizona. (Carol and Doug Allard collection).

BASKET ILLUSTRATIONS WITH IDENTIFICATION

34. Eskimo coiled jar; leather hinge and hasp; ivory ornaments; northern Alaska.

35. Haida basket; plain brown bands; southern Alaska.

36. Aleutian grass-woven ''jar'' in closed twined weave; trade yarn decoration; Aleutian Islands.

37. Aleutian grass-woven ''jar'' in fine open twined weave; trade yarn decoration; Aleutian Islands.

38. Tlingit cooking basket; false embroidery bands; southern Alaska.

39. Burden basket; coiled and imbricated; Thompson River area.

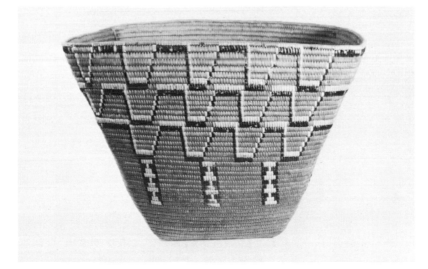

69

40. Nootka plaited basket; Vancouver Island.

41. British Columbia carrying basket; square, coiled weave, false embroidery; with a native woven headband attached.

42. Nootka (Makah) and Salish (Chehalis) picture baskets, twined; northwestern Washington.

43. Klikitat basket; central Washington.

44. Nez Perce "cornshuck bag" (one side); colored yarn decoration; northern Idaho.

45. Nez Perce "cornshuck bag" (other side); colored yarn decoration; northern Idaho.

75

46. Wasco ''sally bags''; northern Oregon.

47. Siletz double handled basket; western Oregon.

48. Pitt River Indian carrying basket; northeastern California.

49. Pomo diagonal twined basket; Russian River and Lake County, California.

50. Pomo lattice weave twined basket; Russian River and Lake County, California.

51. Pomo coiled basket; Russian River and Lake County, California.

52. Pomo feather basket; Russian River and Lake County, California.

53. Washoe coiled basket; Nevada.

83

54. Tulare vertical "rattlesnake" bands; San Joaquin Valley, California.

55. Tulare "friendship" basket; San Joaquin Valley, California.

56. Tulare; typical horizontal ''rattlesnake'' bands; San Joaquin Valley, California.

57. Tulare flat-shouldered jar; ''rattlesnake'' style decoration; San Joaquin Valley, California.

58. Mission basket; concentric stars design; southwestern California.

59. Mission basket; desert palms design; southwestern California.

60. Conejo mission basket; butterfly design — the Conejo were a band of the Diegueno Indians of San Diego County and were extinct by early 1900's; southwestern California.

61. Conejo tribe mission basket; rattlesnake and butterfly design; San Diego County, southwestern California.

62. Mission basket; circus design; southwestern California. (Carol and Doug Allard collection).

63. Apache desert canteen basket, pitched; Arizona/New Mexico.

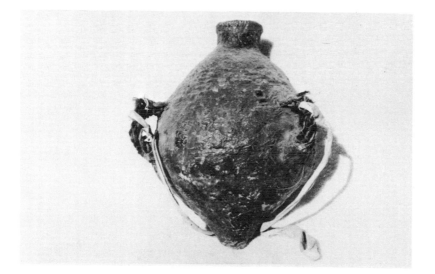

64. Apache "snowflake" design tray; Arizona/New Mexico.

65. Mescalero Apache tray; Texas.

66. Oval Apache basket; Arizona/New Mexico. (Carol and Doug Allard collection).

67. Apache "snowflake" design; Arizona/New Mexico. (Carol and Doug Allard collection).

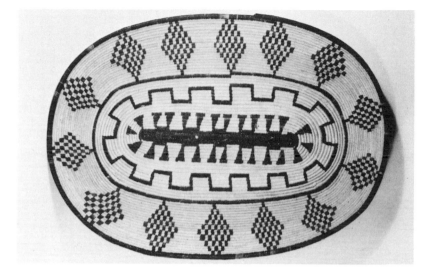

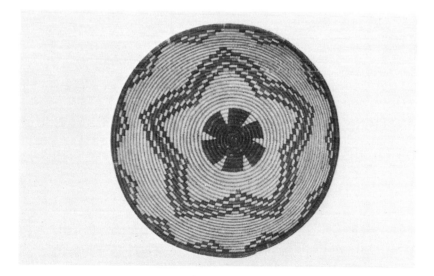

68. Hopi wickerwork tray; Arizona.

69. Pueblo style coil weave bowl; coiling terminated with closed end indicating weaving by a married woman; Arizona/New Mexico.

70. Navajo "wedding basket"; northern Arizona.

71. Pima basket; southern Arizona.

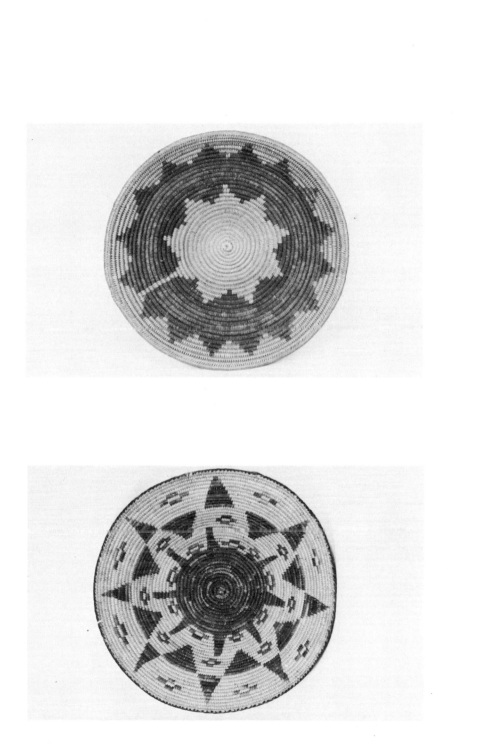

72. Chetimache twilled plaited tray; Louisiana.

73. Papago basket; cactus figure design; southern Arizona.

74. Panamint basket; southeastern California.

75. Umatilla basket; northern Oregon. (Carol and Doug Allard collection).

78. Tlingit cooking pot basket, used; showing wear and tear of such use; was propped up by sand around the sides when in use; southern Alaska.

79. Pine needle coils in a "tourist basket", tribal origin unknown; collected in Montana.

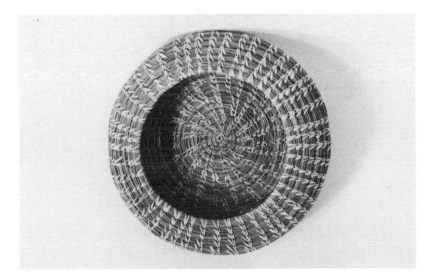

80. Hupa - Yurok - Wyott unfinished cooking basket; warp strands curled around top; northwest California.

81. One of the rare baskets made by the now extinct Chumash Indians of the Santa Barbara area; very few of these baskets survived; coast of southern California.

BASKETRY IN FORMS OTHER THAN BASKETS

82. Kwakiutl harpooner's cape; woven of vegetable fibre, in effect both basketry and cloth textile, like cornshuck bags; design painted on; Vancouver Island.

83. Aleutian wallet, fine as linen but woven with grass; colored silk figures woven in. The finest of all basketry textiles.

113

84. Water jars; tightly twined weaving, heavily pitched; used by Paiute and Southwest Indians and in prehistoric times by Indians of the southern California coast.

85. Grass woven into mitten linings for use by southern Eskimos; adding warmth and inside ventilation.

86. Fish trap made of grape vine in a conical form; Pomo; Russian River and Lake County. A form used by many other Indians and by Eskimos; rare because seldom collected.

87. Eel trap; conical "gate" inside; used by Indians on the coastal rivers of northern California.

88. Winnowing tray; Central Valley California Indians; seeds and grains shaken in the wind when dry were freed of husks, which were blown away; twined weaving.

89. Seed fan or beater; used by Indians to shake and jar seeds from plants; this one Pomo in wicker weave. Russian River and Lake County, California.

119

90. Typical Apache jar; coil weave; chain design with figures, black on white; Arizona/New Mexico.

91. Southern Eskimo jar; coarse soft coil weave with tufts of yarn woven in.

121

92. Paiute baby carrier, woven with a warp of reeds; usual Indian style for full length lash-on; sunshade with symbol for baby boy; Nevada.

93. Wintun (northern California Indian); sit-down baby carrier; child seated on bottom and fastened in.

94. Northwestern California (lower Klamath and Eel River areas) slipper-shaped cradle; baby seated on pocket containing moss; sun shade in place.

95. Western Mono baby cradle; designed for girl; usual Indian style for full length lash-on cradle.

125

96. Lie-down cradle; Northwest Coast style; carried horizontally on woman's back; coil weave, heavily imbricated; British Columbia Indians.

97. Northwest Coast hat; inside view showing cap for head and chin strap; chevron design on brim made by weaving technique.

98. Exterior view of No. 97; painted design of raven in red and black.

99. Mushroom-shaped Northwest Coast hat; cap for head inside; a form familiar in the Orient; totemic design painted in red and black.

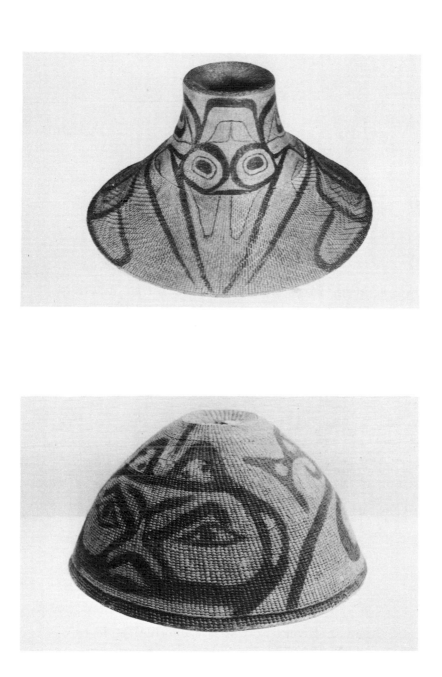

19. Lower Klamath River style of cap-hat; woven in brown and straw colors with design on outer surface only.

101. Upper Klamath River (Northeast California) style cap; black on white; design showing on inside surface.

102. Northeast California cap.

103. Nez Perce cap; northern Idaho. (Carol and Doug Allard collection).

104. Tlingit openwork basket; southern Alaska.

105. Aleutian covered bottle, colored with silk design woven in.

135

106. Nootka (unidentified basketry item).

107. Nez Perce woven ration card pouch decorated with trade beads and old trade cloth; northern Idaho.

137

108. Paiute beaded basket; souvenir type; Nevada.

109. Basketry quiver; twined weave; Klamath tribe; southern Oregon.

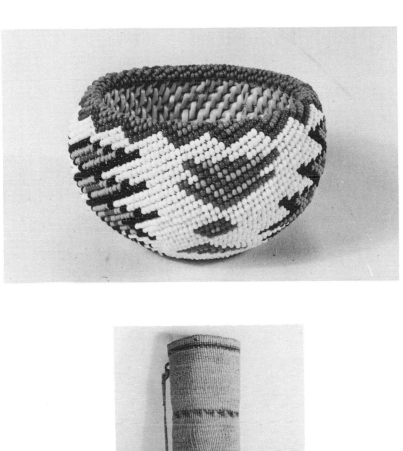

110. Basketry rattle; open twining; probably Klamath tribe; southern Oregon.

111. Braided corn husk coils fashioned into an Iroquois false face mask; New York State.

141

112. Dance basket used in ceremonial dances, perhaps as a wealth symbol, its shape being that of the elk horn purses used by the tribes involved (Hupa/Wyott/Yurok); northwestern California.

113. Basketry sack (25'' long); alternating weft of strands of bark ribbons and root fibre cordage, central weft black yarn, elsewhere root fibre cordage; buckskin rim; perhaps interior British Columbia.

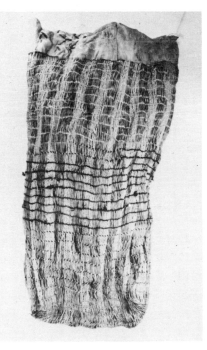

143